The Wonder of
KOALAS

For Ashley and Matt Speer
With special thanks to Barbara Harold
— Kathy Feeney

Please visit our web site at: www.garethstevens.com
For a free color catalog describing Gareth Stevens Publishing's list of high-quality books
and multimedia programs, call 1-800-542-2595 (USA) or 1-800-461-9120 (Canada).
Gareth Stevens Publishing's Fax: (414) 332-3567.

Library of Congress Cataloging-in-Publication Data

Lantier, Patricia.
    The wonder of koalas / by Patricia Lantier and Kathy Feeney; illustrated
by John F. McGee.
       p. cm. — (Animal wonders)
    Includes index.
    "Based on . . . Koala magic for kids . . . by Kathy Feeney"—T.p. verso.
    ISBN 0-8368-2767-8 (lib. bdg.)
    1. Koala—Juvenile literature. [1. Koala.] I. Feeney, Kathy, 1954-
II. McGee, John F., ill. III. Title. IV. Series.
QL737.M384L36 2001
599.2'5—dc21
                                      00-053817

First published in North America in 2001 by
Gareth Stevens Publishing
A World Almanac Education Group Company
330 West Olive Street, Suite 100
Milwaukee, WI 53212 USA

This edition is based on the book *Koalas for Kids,* text © 1999 by Kathy Feeney, with illustrations
by John F. McGee, first published in the United States in 1999 by NorthWord Press, (Creative
Publishing international, Inc.), Minnetonka, MN, and published in a library edition as
Koala Magic for Kids by Gareth Stevens, Inc., in 2000. Additional end matter © 2001 by
Gareth Stevens, Inc.

Photographs © 1999: Erwin & Peggy Bauer: Cover, 12, 15, 16, 20, 26-27, 30, 43; John Shaw: 7, 11,
33, 42; Martin Withers/Dembinsky Photo Associates: 8; Inga Spence/Tom Stack & Associates: 19,
24, 36; Brian Parker/Tom Stack & Associates: 23; Ed Kanze/Dembinsky Photo Associates: 29; Dave
Watts/Tom Stack & Associates: 34, 40; John Cancalosi/Tom Stack & Associates: 39; Art Wolfe: 46.

Printed in the United States of America

1 2 3 4 5 6 7 8 9 05 04 03 02 01

The Wonder of
KOALAS

by Patricia Lantier and Kathy Feeney
Illustrations by John F. McGee

Gareth Stevens Publishing
A WORLD ALMANAC EDUCATION GROUP COMPANY

AUSTRALIA

If you ever visit the island continent of Australia, look high in the trees. You might just see a koala!

Koalas live in eucalyptus trees. They are small, fluffy mammals that look like cuddly teddy bears. But koalas are not bears at all. They are marsupials — like kangaroos.

Koalas are nocturnal animals, so they sleep during the day. At night, they eat. The leaves of eucalyptus trees are their favorite food. Koalas also get the water they need from these leaves. *Koala* is an aboriginal word that means "no drink." The aborigines thought koalas never drank water.

Koalas
have gray
or brown
fur with a
white chin
and chest.
Their
ears are
covered
with long,
fluffy hair.

The fur of a koala blends in well with the bark of eucalyptus trees. They have a spotted rump that also helps them hide in the trees.

Koalas grow to be about 2 feet (0.6 meters) tall. They can weigh up to 30 pounds (14 kilograms).

Koalas look chubby, but they are not fat. They have lean muscles under their fur. A koala's fur changes with the weather. A woolly, waterproof coat keeps the koala warm in winter and dry in rainy weather. In summer, it sheds some of its fur to stay cool.

Koalas
do not
have
tails.
Pear-
shaped
bodies
help
them
balance
on tree
limbs.

Long, powerful arms and legs give koalas the strength they need to climb trees and leap from branch to branch. Koalas would make good Olympic gymnasts!

The front paws of a koala each have two thumbs and three fingers. Each thumb and finger has a sharp, curved claw. The koala's back paws have five toes. Their first toe works like a thumb. It is the only toe without a claw.

Climbing is easy for koalas. They hold onto the trees with their sharp claws, then push themselves up with their strong back legs.

Koalas can climb very high, often 150 feet (46 m). That is like taking an elevator ride to the fifteenth floor of a building!

The branches of eucalyptus trees are like tree houses for koalas. The animals eat in them and sleep in them. Sometimes koalas get so comfortable, they fall asleep while they are still chewing!

Unlike people, koalas can sleep in a tree and not fall out of it. They usually eat and sleep in the same tree for several days. Changing trees takes a long time and a lot of energy.

Since koalas eat only plants, they are called herbivores. Koalas like the leaves of eucalyptus trees best. A koala can eat more than a pound (0.5 kg) of leaves a day. Like squirrels, koalas store food in their cheeks. The stored food comes in handy later on — for a quick snack.

Koalas are picky eaters, but once they find the kind of eucalyptus they like, they eat and eat and eat!

Although eucalyptus leaves are poisonous to most animals, koalas have special stomachs that can digest the leaves' oils. The strong scent of eucalyptus oils protects koalas from fleas and lice. It also gives koalas a sweet smell, like eucalyptus cough drops.

Koalas have powerful jaws with thirty teeth for chewing. Sharp front teeth shred the tough eucalyptus leaves. Flat back teeth mash and grind the leaves so they can be swallowed.

Koalas do not have good eyesight, but they do have good ears and noses for hearing and smelling. When a koala smells danger, it climbs up the nearest tree. Dingoes are probably a koala's greatest danger. A dingo is a reddish-brown wild Australian dog.

Some people think koalas are lazy because they move slowly and sleep at least eighteen hours a day. Actually, koalas do not have much energy because the eucalyptus leaves they eat are not very nutritious. Koalas try to save their energy by moving slowly and sleeping a lot.

Koalas like to be alone. Even when more than one koala climbs the same tree, they will stay away from each other. Koalas spend time with each other only when they are ready to mate or when a mother koala is raising her baby.

Koalas are usually quiet, but they can be very noisy if they have something to say.